Triumph

TRIUMPH

Sarah Flame

All rights reserved. No part of this publication may be reproduced, distributed, or transmitted in any form by any means, including photocopying, recording, or other electronic methods without the prior written permission of the author, except in the case of brief quotations embodied in reviews and certain other noncommercial uses permitted by copyright law. For permission requests, write to the author at the address below.

Copyright © 2022 Sarah Flame
www.sarahflame.com

ISBN 979-8-218-00620-4

Edited and designed by Tell Tell Poetry

Printed in the United States of America

First Printing, 2022

To the mystics, rebels, outsiders, creatives, and pioneers.

To the sisters and brothers who walk
the path of the sacred heart.

To the scar clan who learns to see in the dark,
to speak the unspeakable, finding themselves
both laughing and crying in odd places.

To the road-travellers born to tell a good story by the
fire, longing for a letter to travel across the world.

This one is for you. . . .

CONTENTS

OAK

Sybil	5
Deer Hunt	6
A Favor	7
Rumors	8
Revolution Road	9
Gretchen	10
Heroine Chic	11
Red Fox	12
Mary	13
Captain Jack	14
Amends	15
Cherokee Rose	16
Moonlight	17
Selkie	18

BIRCH

Warrior Horse	21
Shipwreck	22
Ghost Dancer	23
Born of Rattlesnakes	24
Barn Owl	25
Rocky	26
Magdalene	27
Noah's Ark	28
On the Road Again	29
The Runaway	30
Burning Mystic	31
The Rain Washes You Clean	32
Butterfly	33
Indigenous	34

Gypsy	35
Mystery	36
A Good Man	37
Birch Road	38

CEDAR

Wampanoag	41
Triumph	42
Across Lines	43
Robin's Nest	44
Fresh Bread	45
Wolf Keeper	46
Refuge	47
Pear Tree	48
Red Cow	49
Dirty	50
Black Sheep	51
Redemption	52
Aurora	53
Lawbreaker	54
St. Andrew's	55
Gideon Jean	56
Blue Chevy	57
Gambler	58
Jersey Rose	59
Carousel	60
Pearl Coast	61
Sunrise	62

Triumph

OAK

SYBIL

She travels on back roads
a gelding's black mane
pulsing veins
course through the night,
her hands on the reins.

She knocks on every door
with news of the war.
A revolution is near.
Marching footsteps
the sound of cannons
candles in the window
food being stored.

Hounds guarding driveways
storage cellars
vintage coats
herbal oils for the plague.

Maximus bows his head
as she dismounts.
No longer a stranger, she runs.
Burning heart.
Suffragette.

DEER HUNT

One deer
in a field of hunters
who kill what does not live by the rules.

Holding guns—
loaded, ready.

Wincing eyes, target in focus.

She senses danger,
bolts toward the trees.

Missed.

Adrenaline pours down faces.
The rush of a high.
She escapes

her body
a nervous system
of wires
offering songs
to her land.

Reservoirs to drink from.

Holy waters to bathe in.
Gather the people.
Rise again.

A FAVOR

Dear John,

We reached our camp place today near the Great Swamp. Blue and Neda are safe, and we have built a shelter close to the water. We have enough supplies and blankets for two months. I think of you sometimes when I look up at the stars. I heard you made it back to Plymouth and might be heading back north again.

There are rumors we might be in danger from the Calgary men. I miss you, John.

If something happens, I want you to know you are in my heart always—Can you ask your men to watch for us? We might be in danger.

I love you.

Jane Redbear

Narragansett

RUMORS

Tonight the moon is full.

Ancient rocks rest planks on a cabin.

I think of you.

We are dust and flames in a world of rumors.

I found a perfect diamond

broken from years in the ground.

I wore it on my soul
the night when crows circled—
screaming for justice.

This could go on forever.

REVOLUTION ROAD

Footsteps.

Loaded gun barrel.

Why did you leave for the war?

So many days waiting
for your letters—
beautiful skies
birds on branches
sweet fruits on trees
singing doves.

I would walk a block
and watch my letter go
into the postbox
in slow motion

always pausing—

a month
a year
days.

Time—
slow molasses
or beating rain.

I look at the window.

When will you come back?

Davie

GRETCHEN

Inside a Victorian house,
she sat by the window.
A psychic medium
eyes cobalt blue
wearing a velvet robe.
Above her table,
Tiffany stained glass windows.

I remember her words:
earn wisdom,
drink it daily.
She pulled the ace of spades.
There are lots of women going crazy.

For dreams and illusions,
Ophelia drowned herself.

Countless others
in dresses made for princesses
waiting at the door.

Red foxes will surround you in dreams.
Learn to love them
like guardians
waking you from sleep.

Heroine Chic

Thin
sinking willow reed
on the edge of a swamp pool.

Voices of mothers:
Everything all right?

Disappearing
into the darkness
of rooms
with dark angels.
Bad boys.

Signs on doors.

GIRLS

under a spell—

the promise to never grow old.

RED FOX

I text you again:
Are you safe?

The enemy is within me.
So is the savior.

Graceful exits—
the way leaves fall
or trees uproot.

Cyclical bows
in time.

Walking away
or toward
is strength.

Discerning
what is empty
giving from
surrender.

A red fox left pieces of tail fur
on the trailhead.
Offerings from battle.
I hold the sacred pieces
respecting natural law.

Learning what is mine to take
or fight for.

Whose fight?

MARY

You did not want
to take care of anyone
anymore.
Wanting to burn down the house.

Hold the keys.
An innkeeper
with a solid gate.

Drinks for plenty.

Don't you rough up my girls.

CAPTAIN JACK

We set sail in twenty days
expecting rough seas midway.

Heading to the coast of the Atlantic
then down south.

I just want to let you know
if I do not make it back,
I always loved you.

Please remember the day
at Bishops Tavern.

I left you flowers
at your front door.

Much peace,

Captain Jack

AMENDS

I am fifty—
maybe sixty.
I am upstairs,
a door opens.
The sound of footsteps.

Is it you?

There is a table
where I am seated.

I look up.
I spent my whole life
preparing for this moment.
Years working steps.

Upwards, not descending
into destruction.

I was destroyed once.

Years ago
I dreamed of a lion.
Standing at the gates,
a guardian
made a pact.

I crossed a bridge
rising on water.

Black pearl
born from the bottom.

CHEROKEE ROSE

Trails of tears
betrayal
trying to love again
hands shackled
living between imprisonment and life.

A rose opens into the sun,
facing west.
A pierced arrow taken out of the ground
to give something back.
Corn maiden—
arms stretched open
with food and supplies
for everyone.

MOONLIGHT

I dream of the last time
I was with you. . . .

The moon
in the sky.

Like a blessing in time
written in the stars.

If people ask me
I never walked away.

I live
starstruck.

SELKIE

During the last days of fall

I did not know which way to turn.

I was not drifting or walking

aimless.

But then I remembered who I was.

An ancient being
standing at the rocks by the shore.
I remembered the lineage I came from
as the sea roared
with holy tides.

The constellations had names.

BIRCH

WARRIOR HORSE

I want to ride a strong horse today.
I look like the type that can ride
a sensitive rescue
or a gelding with a short gait.
The problem horse in the barn
or the one with the wise-guy act.
The mare that was starved
or the misfit in the herd.

The truth is
I want to feel like a warrior.
To be taken care of
right now.

A battle horse.

It's the part of me
that longs to not be let down
in the time of revolution.
I am riding for my liberty.

SHIPWRECK

I am running so far from you
in your castle of accomplishments,
magnificent gardens.

Holding onto years
of steady hope,
stoic cards.

Can we meet?

The forest is unruly—
full of danger,
broken rules.

The kind of people
I might fall in love with

descending from heights.

Gods to humans.

GHOST DANCER

Inside a tepee,
a fire burns.
There is so much to be
grateful for.

War paint,
holy colors,
strong women
riding mustangs,
brave men supporting
the fallen.

The freedom
of those enslaved.

Dancing wild
under a wolf moon.

May darkness turn to light.

BORN OF RATTLESNAKES

Shedding skin.

Dreaming of rattlesnakes
earth riders
carving ground.
Rising voices
from azure pools.

Below
where we cannot see where we are.
Yet
inside the caves
guiding

trusting
darkness
with lanterns
of illumination.

Starseeds.
Aligning
threads
of creation.
Tapestries,
star constellations.

Maps \ born to live.
Weaving,
honey-dripped.

A time of awakening.

BARN OWL

Molten

owl
on a branch.

High up.

I am learning how to wear
molten feathers.
Extending,
flying downwards.
Huntress with sharp talons
gnawing at the bones.
With eyes into the interior
years of women behind me
wrapped in chains
tearing into the fabric
of societal silence.

Hitting the ground
full speed.
Beating wings.
In flight.

ROCKY

Fist
gloves
ring
beads of sweat.

Punching punch.

Keep going
rising.

Not looking
behind
forward
or back.
Ripped open
in the chest.

Get up
breathing
gasping.

Looking up at the lights—
now stars.
I am out of the race.

A part of,
not against.

MAGDALENE

Red.

The color of many things:

courage
hearts
passion
power
survival.

Wine spilling on the streets
from a silver chalice.

Sarah.
Black Kali.
Her power
was to flee
by boat from Israel.
The gods brought her
to France.
Blue shores
holding oak, roses,
ivy, and tears.

Messengers
from palms releasing
the doves of Magdalene.

Noah's Ark

Fill this boat—
enough food to last for years
in the middle of the sea.

Sending hearts
pearls on a string.

Serenity beads around my neck.
Kissing the sea
leaving behind
a world set on fire.
Riots, forest fires, storms.

I am not escaping,
just going into my heart.
Anchor.

Where is truth and justice?
Will you travel far?

ON THE ROAD AGAIN

Dear Sarah,

Did I ever tell you the road cures my soul?
It's freedom. The phone shuts off; texts slow down.
I see the island of everyone way behind me.
No one knows me, so I can be who I want to be.
I can be a changed man.
Don't get me wrong—I can have fun.
Fun is what it is all about.
You are a brave lady.

Keep writing.
I will read your new one. I got some time now.

Triumph.
Right?

Well anyway,
you understand.
Call me sometime.

Always my best,

Gideon Jean

THE RUNAWAY

The sun cracks open the sky
like a chisel into the ground.
I am rocking a child
in my heart.
Ghosts that live here,
their shovels dig deep
into the soil.
A rich brown to birth
harvests of yellow marigold.

Will you stay this time?

She faces
the cherry tree,
kneeling in mercy.
The bark
of an ancient shroud.
Lifting itself
into the essence of blue star.
Holding soft whiteness
so the petals embrace the wind
and sky with new life.

They called her a runaway
to keep running.

She yearned for kindness.

BURNING MYSTIC

Burning mystics.
A collective in your heart.

Sometimes you need to leave everything
for your freedom.

Creative soul.

You know you do not fit into the pack
trying to turn pain into pleasure.

Turn inward,
bitter or stung.

It is your turn
to grow
your soul—
salt, stones, and earth.

This life is yours.

THE RAIN WASHES YOU CLEAN

I am hearing a blessing,
the rain wet on my skin.
Taking all the hatred,
bitterness, and resentment
back to the source.

I can't carry this.
It is not mine.

Alone.

Maybe our meetings
were accidental designs
or forced arrangements.
Holy.
Profane.

It does not really matter now.
I am on a search for what is real.
Willing to break my shell.
A child of God.

BUTTERFLY

Blue morpho
butterfly
inside my throat.
Ruby ray

extending
from my third eye,
glowing.

I am called to speak
as a revolution
draws closer.

Eyes glisten.
Rain cleanses
my face.
Waves crash
and divisions wage.
Underneath the waves,
the gates of my heart
open.

World on fire
set aflame.

Hands stretch open
offering
love's awakening.

INDIGENOUS

Over time
I grew my hair long
wore beaded earrings.
Face bare
staring boldly.
Carrying
the energy of trees
lying on top of deep roots.
Walking barefoot on rocks
by the lakeshore.

One day
I walked to Taughannock Falls
taking my drum into the canyon.

Felt how big I was
inside the echoes
of an earth cathedral.

It was not easy
reclaiming
fierce love.

GYPSY

She taught me to love
orphans
rescue animals
blooming flowers
big scarves
wild jewelry.

She kept me close to a creative fire.

Her black Cadillac had red velvet seats
with tinted windows.
Bohemian stained lipsticks
amethyst nail polish
scented perfumes.
Red wine with
Italian labels.

High heels that clicked the ground.

Click click click.

Her words of wisdom
in a candle-dripped letter.

Your power is within you.

MYSTERY

The lake sits behind me
as trees glisten with icicles.
A stone castle
like the one in Tallinn.
A medieval city
the birthplace of seven generations
of my mother's family.

Estonia
the Orlov horses
a lake on our farm
with a long, windy driveway
at the end,
a sign:

Auksi Farm.

She lost her city.
A battle to occupy
a small country by the sea
by invaders from two directions.

Folk is what she passed onto me.
Sami fur coats
trails in the snow,
her old piano.
Fireplaces lit.
Flowers and herbs
made into hot teas
held in emerald cups.

Something was not broken in the feminine.
I carry the memory of singers
in my bones.

A GOOD MAN

Bobby picked me up in his pickup truck.

My car broke down
in front of 91 East.

I had a bad feeling
like anything could happen.
But I was a strong woman.
I could look scary too.

*A rebel with black hair
or a witch with a broom.
A dangerous crazy lady
forbidden or angry.*

I wanted to climb in his seat,
coffee on the right side.
A smile for comfort.

Acceptance is a river
we all turn to.
Sacred bonds
woven in threads of trust
not dictated by outdated codes
or law books.

Love reaching outwards.

No matter what.

BIRCH ROAD

Dear Manny,

I made it to Washington. I drove miles, my body ragged and tired. I lost two horses, Star and Jace. I could not get them to safety with the floods and the war raging. When I got to Cree Walker's camp, I fell on an old birch tree. I have searched for months for this tree. Sometimes the feeling of belonging is found in the stars, the plants, and the ground. I feel at home in nature while my family is all dislocated. John Cray raided my sister's house, then stole her jewelry and her dresses for his new wife, Claudia. I saw the broken door and his pickup truck leaving the driveway. I am sure Claudia will look beautiful in that dress, all dolled up at Sunday Pickett's church day. I saw myself in the mirror the other day. I looked like the picture of the natives they call *savages*—my hair wild, eyes as black as night. For the first time, I saw my beauty. I have been searching for so long. I felt the earth loving me. I guess I felt your love too.

Love,

Reindeer Song

CEDAR

WAMPANOAG

On the banks
of the Eel River,
months carving tree boats,
burning smoke
day in and day out,
winter came.
Many died
clutching fur skins—
souls of animals, totems
willing to offer warmth.

A signed letter
with ink drying.

We proclaim the rights of your land.

Ancestors dance
in rhythm.

This time is ours.

TRIUMPH

Part of the earth
animal kingdom
plant kingdom
universe.

We inherited this world.
Caught with one foot
in the noose.
Playing with time and territory.

Chin up, soldiers,
pilgrims of a new land.
Each wearing a number,
being counted in the herd.

I live
to live.

Studying the intersection between
ownership and freedom.

ACROSS LINES

Warrior paint.
Generational lines.
Mixed ink.

Red, brown, yellow, white.
The world rumbles with fires and ceremony.
Ghost dancers are being raised
from the ground,
standing in the enemy's territory.

A new stance
born from kindness.
Webs of connection
thriving
across lines
without trespassing.

Holding on
to love.

Gather the food.
Harvest.
The star cloak of Guadalupe.
Wreaths of ivy.

Bees weaving honey
geometric shapes
of wholeness
into life.

ROBIN'S NEST

I came to safety—
a chance to feel reborn again.
I know the stars shine
the moon glows
deer take their young to water.

Lost tracks
footprints.

I deserve this life,
flowers, water, and air.
Earth beneath me
a white canvas to paint on
roses that drench my soul.

I am learning this
life is mine
the hard way.

Years of gambling men
the promise
of a few days.
Will you return?

Love is too expansive.
Its limitless potential.

Her medicine pipe glows.
I will guide you out of this mess
to be free.

Again.

Did we inherit the earth?
Harvest gold.
Soul shining life.

FRESH BREAD

Matthew greeted me,
his brown eyes
gateways to the scriptures
from the living.
I told him my name was Sarah.
I'd just arrived.

Which way to Plymouth plantation?
Eel bank
where the natives lived.
Did the ships come in last night?
Midnight
waves breaking.

The first peoples
touched stone.
While a woman sails in a carved birch boat.
Her home is on the periphery—
brown skin
sunflowers in her heart.

Hundred years houses left.
Survival is buried deep in the ground.
Related?

WOLF KEEPER

She lived in the woods
in a cabin by the lake
holding onto the old ways.
*Teas, herbs, candles,
and salves.*

They called her healer.

With her
wolves in the woods
a circle of protection
guardians of her tale.

Bighearted lady,
her voice had
might.

Too strong for some
broken by a big laugh
to remember.

Tell her story.
She is
living proof
of her life.

REFUGE

A sanctuary is built from tall trees.
Guardian rocks.

There is a revolution going on.

Divisions of us and them.

A temple of pines.
Humble
in knowing its place.

I fall in love with ashen dirt.
The beauty of who we are
in truth.

Belonging.

PEAR TREE

I am sitting close to the roots
of a tree facing Cayuga Lake.

Pears fall to the ground.
Abundant blessings.

Turquoise-blue water.
Fish swimming close
to the currents.

Traces of the American dream.

Whose dream?

Settlers bought up the towns, lands.
Papers changed hands.
Signatures signed
judges as witnesses.
Ownership and power.
Territories declared
as natives moved out.

What is remembered or forgotten?

The lights of windows lit.

Candles burning.
Engraved with sacred hoops

of those who lived and died.

Faith
etched in the stars.

RED COW

Her coat silky red
standing
hooves digging into dirt.

Years of being bought and sold
chattel for work.
Her body
marked with hot iron.

Aging
off the market
she grows into her new place
surrounded by trees.

Lasting one hundred years
on the earth
passing owners.

Red Cow.
Mother of red dirt.

DIRTY

Wrinkles
rough skin
hard living.

Travel up the coast
to Canada.
Deep in the forests
camping with fires.
Eating trout from the rivers
playing guitars till sunrise.

Hands dirty.

In a few days
back to work
on Devil Island.

Barter for dreams.
Nothing is the same
while standing still.

Forgetting is priceless.

BLACK SHEEP

Dear Harriet,

It's been years since I talked to you. *It's hard to find the words.* I saw Bertha last week, and she still misses John and the kids. I wish I could have warned her not to move to that small town with two adopted Black kids. How would she manage with a small family unit and a mostly Quaker town? She started them in church and later had to drop out because they were not fitting in with the other kids. One day, Desy came back crying. One of the girls put gum in her hair and locked her in the closet. She came back home in tears. . . . She could not do her schoolwork after that. I don't know what to say about what happened, just that it's so hard to find the words now. We all loved Desy. . . . I know we can never meet again. I was in that town, and it's too hard to find a bridge of hope, or faith, to any resolution. *Sometimes people try to make what can never be right into . . . what could be? I don't know how or why that's so.* . . . Harriet, are you well?

Blessings,

Birdsong

REDEMPTION

Water hits my face
every morning.
I look out the window.
Nothing is the same
as yesterday.
My head turns backwards
to the past.

A mess of snakes.
Fires torching roads.
Burnt bridges.
Silent, buried,
angry words.

In the mirror
I am softening my eyes.
Remembering
a schoolteacher's voice.

You must be kind.

Yes.

No longer blinded.

AURORA

Miles of corn plains
dairy farms.
Upstate New York.
Aurora

Counting eggs
sheep.
Planning for the future.
Waves from Cayuga Lake.
Ripple.

I offer prayers to a tree
a visitor from out of town.

A history of battles.
Betrayals, war,
now blue skies
golden harvest.
A lake glistens.
Everything resurrected.
Healed in time.
Dead trees recycle
seeds planted
in seasons.

Patience.

Not trespassing or disrupting the fallen
grounds of living peace warriors.

LAWBREAKER

Posted March 29.

Driving on Route 7
trucks on the side of the road.
Many wanted plates.
Lawbreakers.

My eyes shot open at the wheel.
I can understand the rage and grief
caught on Earth.
Memories.
Years ago
laughing at Joe's Pizza.
Closed down/
signs.

I am
learning to trust something higher,
tired of fear.

Just past Kent, I saw an owl lift out of a tree.
Big brown wings of gold and white.
The river felt like a force of nature.
Fate.

I have to remember how we are all connected.
The power to force anything
is not ours anymore.

I wonder if I will ever see you.
Are you alive?

Love,
Butterfly

ST. ANDREW'S

Cavalry Horses engraved
on stained windows.
I am on the phone with you
wrestling love versus religion.

I am not your enemy.
The church has not cast me out
or sent me to hell.

Love is too big
for these narrow halls.

Why did you numb your heart?

Everything heals.

GIDEON JEAN

I often wondered
what happened

to Gideon Jean.

Mean as steel
to protect
a heart so pure
to begin with.

Hardness is not born into.
Sometimes it's just a response
to a world that continually wants
something.

Gideon Jean.

The rebel
living in my heart.

BLUE CHEVY

A sunny day.
Bobby picked me up for ice cream.

A melted cone.
I remember the time
I tried to catch a rabbit
in the park.

I wanted to hold the vulnerable,
soft, timid, sensitive, afraid.
For years, predators seemed like charmers.

Until pictures of girls
appeared.
Hidden like secrets
with no needs
just dreams.

Breaking free.

No longer prey.

It took a tribe of elders,
medicine women,
burning letters and sage.

No more.

GAMBLER

All the women in town
fell for Lukas.

A gambling man.
He drove a blue truck
with a loud muffler.
Sometimes wore his baseball cap
backwards
with a sideways grin.

C'mon, sweetheart,
I'll buy you lunch.
Maybe dinner?

He lived in an old trailer
down Birds Hawk Road.
Girls would follow him
into mystery and danger.
He wanted to steal the world.
Every game was worth playing.

One day his truck disappeared.

Freedom.
Stars filled the night.
The road now his.

JERSEY ROSE

When the night broke its tide,

I opened my eyes.
Sunlight shined from many hearts.
A key to a silver Chevy,
yellow plates.

Jersey Rose.

To a gypsy heart.

Be free.

CAROUSEL

Wind in my hair
head tilted back
riding a copper horse
cascading mane.

A horse of my own.

Looking upwards
to the sky.
I belong to me.

Worthy of the emerald in my heart,
the depth of protection.

Gem of the earth.

PEARL COAST

Oyster mirror.

Shells from the sea
salty hair
abalone shells
smoke from sage.

Clear this land

for the people.

From the sea,
legends emerge.
A tribe of many who came
to settle by the shores.

An abundant earth
not dry
or diminished.

SUNRISE

I woke today
with flowers and honey on the table.
Bees circled the window
as a reminder of harmony.
The strength of what remains.

Born a dark horse
in front of a carriage.
Riding with spirit pulsing in my veins,
fighting for love to be sweeter.
Inside of sunlight

shining behind clouds and rain.

About the Author

Sarah Flame is a Bhakti writer devoted to raising consciousness in the feminine emergence movement. Her work is rooted in an embodiment of the natural world, animal communication, and service to the earth. She loves art, mysticism, horses, shamanism, and being part of a community of creative visionaries. Her poetry is an offering and reflection towards beauty and the divine.

www.ingramcontent.com/pod-product-compliance
Lightning Source LLC
Chambersburg PA
CBHW031639160426

43196CB00006B/475